It's Sukkah Time!

Latifa Berry Kropf

photographs by Tod Cohen

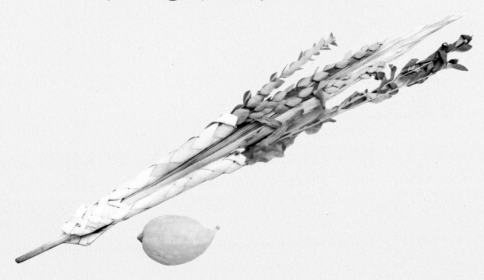

KAR-BEN
PUBLISHING

Thanks to Congregation Beth Israel Preschool...

To the staff for their flexibility and enthusiasm, to the parents for their wonderful children, to the children who bring me so much joy.

To my children, Elizabeth and Michael, for being the sweet fragrance in my life, and to my husband Peter, my Sukkat Shalom.

L.B.K.

About Sukkot:

Sukkot is a fall holiday that celebrates the harvest and recalls the Jewish people's wandering in the desert after the Exodus. The sukkah (plural, sukkot), a temporary dwelling, is akin to the huts farmers lived in during the harvest, as well as the shelters the Jewish travelers built in the desert. The roof of the sukkah is covered with branches and its walls are decorated with colorful fruits and vegetables to commemorate the harvest. Families eat, study, and sometimes sleep in the sukkah. We bless the etrog (a citrus fruit) and shake the branches of the lulav (a palm frond bound with branches of myrtle and willow) to thank God for all things that grow.

Text copyright © 2004 by Latifa Berry Kropf
Photos copyright © 2004 by Tod Cohen

KAR-BEN PUBLISHING, INC.
A division of Lerner Publishing Group
241 First Avenue North
Minneapolis, MN 55401 U.S.A.
800-4KARBEN

Website address: www.karben.com

Library of Congress Cataloging-in-Publication Data

Kropf, Latifa Berry.
    It's sukkah time / by Latifa Berry Kropf ; photographs
by Tod Cohen.
        p.   cm.
    Summary: Photographs show and text describes children creating and celebrating in a sukkah, a harvest booth built to celebrate the Jewish holiday of Sukkot.
    ISBN: 1–58013–084–4 (lib. bdg. : alk. paper)
    1. Sukkot—Juvenile literature. [1. Sukkot. 2. Holidays.]
I. Cohen, Tod, ill. II. Title.
BM695.S8K74 2002
296.4'33—dc21   2002156662

Manufactured in the United States of America
2 3 4 5 6 7 – JR – 09 08 07 06 05 04

Sukkot celebrates the harvest.
It comes in autumn when the leaves fall...

and apples and pumpkins...

are ripe and ready to pick.

It's time to build our sukkah.
We connect the boards,
tighten the screws...

and lift the frame up high.

Michael and Tali are stringing colored beads
and pasta to decorate our sukkah.

Look at Ruby's silly fingers!

Let's make a sukkah for our classroom, too.

How many of us can fit inside?

We can even make little sukkot…

just the right size for our toy people.

Our teacher helps us decorate the sukkah.

When we hang the chains
we can see the sky through the roof.

The sukkah is done! It's time to celebrate.
Let's sing...

and dance…

and have some snacks.

It's fun to eat in the sukkah!

The lemony etrog reminds us of the harvest.
It smells sweet.

We shake the branches of the lulav in all
directions to show that God is everywhere.

Sometimes it rains on Sukkot,
but we don't mind. Rain means
there will be a good harvest next year.

Little Sukkot

What you need:

Plastic fruit or veggie baskets
   with a "door" cut out
Pipe cleaners cut to 3"–4" lengths
Plastic beads or macaroni with large holes*
Small plastic fruits and vegetables, and
   strips of leaves and berries (found in
   craft stores)

Paper plates or mat board to
   place under sukkot
Glue

*For children over 3

What you do:

String beads or macaroni on pipe cleaners.
Bend at one end to hold them on.
Attach to sukkah.
Cut lengths of fall leaves and weave through the baskets.
Glue on plastic fruits and vegetables.

Note: *Older children may want to decorate the inside of their sukkot before decorating the roof. Small pieces of paper, markers and colored pencils can be used to make pictures or blessings. Modeling clay, card stock, and pieces of fabric can be used to make miniature furniture, lulav and etrog, and candlesticks.*

SUKKOT BLESSINGS

Sitting in the Sukkah

בָּרוּךְ אַתָּה יְיָ אֱלֹהֵינוּ מֶלֶךְ הָעוֹלָם,
אֲשֶׁר קִדְּשָׁנוּ בְּמִצְוֹתָיו וְצִוָּנוּ לֵישֵׁב בַּסֻּכָּה.

Baruch Atah Adonai Eloheinu Melech ha'olam,
Asher kid'shanu b'mitzvotav v'tzivanu leshev basukkah.

Thank You, God, for the mitzvah of dwelling in the sukkah.

Lulav and Etrog
Hold the lulav in your right hand and the etrog in your left hand. The stem of
the etrog should be pointing up, and the lulav and etrog should be touching.

בָּרוּךְ אַתָּה יְיָ אֱלֹהֵינוּ מֶלֶךְ הָעוֹלָם,
אֲשֶׁר קִדְּשָׁנוּ בְּמִצְוֹתָיו וְצִוָּנוּ עַל נְטִילַת לוּלָב.

Baruch Atah Adonai Eloheinu Melech ha'olam,
Asher kid'shanu b'mitzvotav v'tzivanu al n'tilat lulav.

Thank You, God, for these fragrant fruits of the harvest,
for the sun and rain which make them grow,
for the seasons of nature and the seasons of our lives.

After the blessing, turn the etrog so the stem is pointing down.
Wave the lulav and etrog together in all directions—north, south, east, west, up, and down.